Goodbye, Leinster House
Fake Façade of Democracy

Joe Curtis

First Edition 2019

First Return Press
11 Park Avenue
Dublin 16
Ireland

Distributed by Amazon

ISBN: 9781088928394

Cover photograph: 2019 photo of Leinster House, Dublin, during refurbishment.

Democracy or veiled dictatorship?

The present system

As citizens, we can select our President, who is merely an expensive figurehead, and has no actual power. Yet we are not allowed to vote for and directly elect our Taoiseach (Prime Minister), who wields real power. Nor are we allowed to directly elect the other Ministers, who also have great power. We have absolutely no say in who becomes a Minister of State, or a Junior Minister, or a Special Adviser to a Minister. We do not select the top civil servants, who in reality run the country on a day-to-day basis, and exercise great influence over politicians, either by act or omission.

We vote for a bunch of self-nominated politicians, but we have no control over who will occupy the various ministries. Usually, the leader of the political party which gets the most seats automatically becomes Taoiseach, and then he alone decides on the various ministries. He can also re-shuffle the ministries while in power. If there is a change in leadership of the major party during the term of office, he or she automatically become Taoiseach, without any input whatsoever from the citizens of the country. This is exactly what happened in recent years, when Taoiseach Enda Kenny retired, and Leo Varadkar assumed the role of Taoiseach. In effect, the Taoiseach is an un-elected dictator. Is it any wonder that the people of Ireland are sick and tired of politics and politicians?

Ireland has two Houses of Parliament, the un-elected Seanad and the elected Dail. The ultimate power is vested in only a few members of the Dail, and the Seanad merely functions as an expensive "talking shop". The members of the Seanad are not democratically elected by the voters of Ireland, but instead are nominated by the Taoiseach and a few select educational and similar bodies.

The Dail has 160 members, generally half in power, and half in opposition. In reality, only the Taoiseach and Ministers have the power, and the vast bulk of the Dail members do nothing whatsoever, and occasionally turn up for a useless debate, or a bit of a good-humoured banter, just to get their faces on television.

As a small nation, we can and should do an awful lot better in the way we run our country and manage our affairs. Some multi-national companies are bigger than the Irish economy, and are efficiently run by a handful of well-educated, experienced and hard-working executives. We don't need hundreds of politicians and hundreds of thousands of civil servants to manage out tiny island nation.

What is genuine democracy?

A democratic nation is one where all the people are governed by a system that is chosen and controlled by all the citizens, by way of elections and referenda. By "all the citizens" we mean a majority of citizens. In Ireland, the system was written down in the Constitution in 1922, and again in 1937, and has been amended numerous times since then. However, it should be noted that the 1937 Constitution was voted upon in a Referendum, where 57% voted in favour, and 43% against, and therefore that Constitution doesn't really reflect the wishes of all the citizens.

Now, on the eve of the centenary of the official founding of the state in 1922, it is time for the present generation of better-educated citizens to choose and implement a new Constitution.

Firstly, we have to ask ourselves what exactly is the meaning of "the will of the people". When we talk about all the citizens, we have to acknowledge that not everyone is interested in how the State is run, and some prefer to concentrate on their own lives. Others are interested, but do not like the present system, and opt not to participate in elections. Some do not like any of the candidates, and stay away from the polling booths. There are also those citizens, who do not like the system nor candidates for election, but nevertheless choose to vote, simply as a way of "exercising their democratic right"! Some even go along just to make a "spoilt vote". Hence, turnout at elections can be poor on occasions. However, when turnout is constantly below 50% of the electorate, there is something drastically wrong, and that is precisely the situation in Ireland.

A fundamental issue is what constitutes a "majority", and in Ireland it means more that 50% of the votes (in theory, one extra citizen!). This is totally unacceptable in a civilised society, because it means that, potentially, almost 50% of the citizens have no say in the running of the state. A majority should be a high percentage, possibly 90%, 75%, etc, but a reasonable compromise would be 66.66% or more, i.e. over two-thirds of votes. This is not a magic number, and even 66% would be common sense. However, for extremely important issues, 75% of the votes might be necessary.

The next question of importance is the notion of "one person, one vote". The present system of the "single transferable vote" does not represent this fundamental right, since it results in some candidates being elected against the overall will of the people. Frequently, political parties obtain more seats than warranted by their percentage of the vote. The fairest system is for the candidate with the most votes to be elected, i.e. "first past the post". If we want to give citizens more choice, this could be limited to a maximum of three options, but sub-dividing the single vote into two or three parts. For example, vote for only one candidate (100%), or vote for two candidates (66.67% for the favourite, 33.33% for the second choice), or vote for three candidates (50% for favourite, 33.34% for second choice, and 16.66% for third choice).

The 1990 presidential election shows how foolish the "Quota" and "transferable vote" is, since Brian Lenihan had the most votes of all candidates (694,484 against Mary Robinson's 612,265 first preference votes), yet Mary Robinson became President. President Higgins was elected for a second term in 2018, simply because there was a poor selection of candidates offered to the electorate.

Politician

What exactly is a politician? Do children say that they would like to be a politician when they grow up? Are they people who have failed at or dislike their chosen professions? Or are they too lazy to continue their original occupation? Is a politician someone interested in State policies? Someone interested in power and status? Someone interested in how a country is governed on a daily basis? Someone who cannot stop talking, and loves the sound of his own voice, or adores debates and being argumentative? In most cases, a politician tends to be a mixture of all the foregoing.

In conversation, we sometimes say that another person would make a good politician, because they will never give you a straight answer, nor express a particular opinion. Sometimes, they behave in this manner, because in reality, they do not know the answer to a question, or have no opinions on a particular subject, but are afraid to admit their weaknesses. At other times, they want to keep all their options open, and are waiting to find out what the general consensus is, before deciding that they will do the same as most other people.

In truth then, a politician is a weak and shallow person, very untrustworthy, and not the sort of person who should be running a country, enacting new legislation, or making decisions about the best interests of the citizens.

Political Parties

A political party is a small group of selfish citizens, belonging to a private club, who title themselves politicians, who think they know best, and seek to manipulate the general public, firstly to implement their particular policies, and secondly to obtain power, prestige and reward for themselves. In general, they attract people who are allergic to a hard day's work, have "notions of grandeur", and have "the gift of the gab". Most are not trained to manage a country, and many have inadequate education, or experience, or both.

Political parties are effectively secret societies, but funded from public money. Any "Tom, Dick or Harry" can set up a political party, and receive state financial aid to running the party, although the State has no control over the party! The membership amounts to only a tiny percentage of the population, and foolish unpaid members (canvassers) do most of the work at election time, in order to get the senior members into government. The party selects a candidate for election, without any input from the majority of citizens, and then expects the voters to elect them to high office! How absolutely ridiculous is that? Candidates rarely turn up at people's houses, and never have their curriculum vitae (CV) with them, only a glossy leaflet with silly slogans and false promises. The childish activity of putting up election posters shows what politicians think of the electorate – mindless sheep. To cap it all, taxpayers pay for politician's Constituency offices and a Secretary.

Political parties may have been inevitable in 1922 when Ireland was polarised between Catholic and Protestant, landlord and tenant, Home Rule or Unionist, etc. It must also be remembered that the 1922 Treaty was only ratified on a bare majority, with 64 votes in favour and 57 votes against, which does not equate even to a 66.66% majority, let alone a 75% majority which would probably be more appropriate for such a major political decision.

When the prospective leaders of the new State should have spoken with one voice, and co-operated for the common good, they started to fight amongst themselves, specifically in order to create two parties. Hence, the citizens were drawn into a bloody civil war, and for decades afterwards felt obliged to support one or other of the two major political parties. This loyalty was passed from generation to generation, with families proudly proclaiming that their parents always voted for such and such party, even if the candidates were disliked or even fools.

Nearly a century later, most people have forgotten the Civil War, and none of the political parties have anything to offer, in terms of improving the country and its citizens. Glossy policy brochures may be circulated, but are quickly ignored when the election is over. The biggest joke is to promise lower taxes, in effect telling the hard-working taxpayer that the State will forcibly take a big chunk of his wages, and might give him back a tiny slice of his own money! The next joke is to promise an increase in capital spending, again using the tax-payers money, when in fact the intention is to build roundabouts or art galleries in politicians own back-yards, to the detriment of the common-good and strategic national planning. In reality, politicians have nothing to give, and would never dream of digging into their own pockets in the national interest. Rural politicians are only interested in petty local constituency issues, and have no knowledge or interest in national issues, nor the greater good. All politicians have a very limited local mandate to make laws for the country, instead of having a national mandate. Politicians do not represent their constituents even on some issues. They are supposed to be neutral or impartial, yet opt to follow their conscience on some moral issues, even though they were not elected on such grounds, and do not have the national interest at heart.

Only the media partially holds the Government to account. Opposition parties don't rock the boat, since they will probably be back in power at the next election. In the current Parliament, there is no opposition at all, with the two main parties scratching each other's back, in a so-called "confidence & supply agreement! Does it require 166 politicians to make simple decisions? However, the media is not faultless, since it also promotes the interests of politicians by giving them free "air-time" or printed columns, whereas the candidates should have to satisfy a strong interview board. Some parties are only voted into power, in order to get another party out, as happened after the Property Crash of 2008.

Even the two main political parties are not guaranteed the lions share of the seats in the Dail at each alternate election. When a coalition becomes necessary, the electorate has absolutely no say in the make-up of the Government, which eventually emerges after a lot of un-democratic "horse-dealing". The recent tendency for Independents to hold the "balance of power" and blackmail the country, is completely un-democratic. In the 2016 election, some Independents even were given Ministerial posts, despite having little or no political experience. Furthermore, "single-issue" candidates should not be allowed in a national Parliament which deals with multiple issues of national importance.

The only people who effectively elect the Prime Minister, are the few thousand local people who voted for him or her. The voters of some local constituency, often in some remote part of the country, have no knowledge or interest in what happens in the rest of the country, yet are the only ones to elect maybe the Prime Minister or some other crucial Minister.

There is greater voter turnout for Referenda in urban areas, where there are more well-educated voters, and greater turnout in elections in rural areas, because the former addresses national issues, and the latter only represents parochial issues.

In short, political parties are a serious and unacceptable threat to democracy.

How to change the present status-quo?

We can expect no sympathy from the existing crop of politicians and civil servants, since effectively, they would be voting themselves out of a job. As an example, a few years ago, the lack-lustre Fine Gael political party, having been voted into power as a punishment to the outgoing self-serving Fianna Fail party, promised to abolish the Seanad (the useless Upper House), but failed to honour their word.

In other countries, political change only came about through bloody revolutions and civil wars. But the Irish are a passive and peaceful people, and many voters, especially in rural Ireland, may be quite content with the present political system, despite all its faults.

Therefore, the introduction of a radically new Constitution will be very difficult, and may have to be done in small gradual stages.

The present trend for Independent politicians could be encouraged, firstly as a way of diminishing the power of political parties, and secondly, to cause maximum mayhem in the Dail, where everyone is at loggerheads, and no work is done. If the Dail were to be completely full of Independents, the voting public would see what a circus the Dail really is. Then maybe there would be more appetite to adopt a completely new Constitution and method of governing the country.

Mass boycotting of elections by voters may be an effective method of forcing change. Likewise, huge numbers of "spoilt" votes may cast doubt on the constitutionality of electing politicians who received only a few hundred votes each.

However, great change could be achieved even by two simple amendments to the existing Constitution, namely:

(a) Declaring that a "majority" means at least 66.66% of votes.

(b)   Abandoning the badly titled "proportional representation" system of voting, and introducing the "first past the post" system, linked to a logical interpretation of "one person, one divisible vote".

Ireland in 2019 is a dynamic and progressive country, not because of the archaic system of government, or the poor calibre of politicians and civil servants, but because of the hard work, talent, vision, love of country, and high calibre of the people who are governed. These are the people who will modernise Ireland.

Finally, what is to become of Leinster House, the seat of the present system of government, after Portlaoise becomes the political capital of Ireland? Very simple. The building will be ideal additional quarters for the adjoining National Library, National Museum, National Gallery, and also for the National Archives, as a fitting epitaph for an institution consigned to history. It will be particularly nice for the main branch of the National Museum to be moved out of the totally-unsuitable Collins Barracks, and for the latter site to be flattened and used to build attractive social housing.

Hopefully, saying "Good-bye" to Leinster House will not be the usual long-winded affair so beloved of Irish party-goers!

Proposed new Constitution

The following draft constitution is an attempt to shake off the original constitution which was imposed on the battle-weary citizens of Ireland 100 years ago, and to start afresh in the best interests of the new and better-educated generations of Irish citizens. The main provisions are in bold type, and the ordinary text represents comments and possible explanations.

Proposed 2022 Constitution of Ireland

(1st Draft)

Meaning of Constitution

1. This document is the fundamental legal framework of Ireland, laying down the duties and rights of the citizens, how the country is governed and managed, how the country is financed, how laws are made, and how law and order is maintained.

General Description of Ireland

2. Ireland comprises the counties of Carlow, Cavan, Clare, Cork, Donegal, Dublin, Galway, Kerry, Kildare, Kilkenny, Laois, Leitrim, Limerick, Longford, Louth, Mayo, Meath, Monaghan, Offaly, Sligo, Roscommon, Tipperary, Waterford, Westmeath, Wexford, Wicklow, on the island

of Ireland, including the seas around the land, the earth beneath the land, and the airspace above the land.

Northern Ireland holds no interest for the younger generations today.

3. Irish people are those born and reared for at least ten years in Ireland. Immigrants living in Ireland for at least fifteen years may apply for Irish nationality, if they have no criminal record in Ireland or another country, in addition to being able to read, write and speak English.

Thousands of asylum seekers are currently held in "direct provision centres" for many years, which effectively are like "prisoner-of-war camps". This is a scandal of international proportions, and is a serious black stain on Ireland's reputation.

4. The official language of Ireland is English. As members of the European Union, French, German, Spanish, Italian, and other European languages are strongly fostered in the education system.

Irish is a dead language, and should not be taught in school, or used in official documents, street signs, etc.

5. The national flag of Ireland is coloured green, white and orange, in three equal vertical strips, with green on the inner side, white in the centre, and orange on the outer side.

6. The national anthem of Ireland is the chorus of "The Soldier's Song", written by Peadar Kearney, with music by Patrick Heeney, as follows:

"Soldiers are we, whose lives are pledged to Ireland, some have come, from a land beyond the wave, sworn to be free, no more our ancient sireland, shall shelter the despot or the slave, tonight we man the "bearna bhaoil", in Erin's cause, come woe or weal, mid cannon's roar and rifle's peal, we'll chant a soldier's song."

The words can be changed by referendum, but not the music.

Most Irish people do not know the Irish words, and might not like the military tone of the actual English words. However, the air or tune is ingrained in the Irish consciousness.

7. The national symbol of Ireland is the Irish harp, with 14 strings.

Guinness also uses the harp as its trademark, so the number of strings in the Irish harp needs to be specified.

8. There is no national religion in Ireland.

Religion is a very private matter, and should not be state-supported or sponsored. It should not be regarded as a charity, and organisations should not be tax-exempt. At present, the State gives the Catholic Church, and presumably other churches, millions of euros every year, since it allows the church to claw back tax-relief on parishioners Easter and Christmas "dues", money collections during Mass, etc. The church accountants ask parishioners to sign a tax claim form every year, stating that at least €250 euros has been donated to charity (i.e. the church).

9. Dublin is the cultural capital city, where the national museum, national gallery, national library, national archives, etc are located.

10.   Portlaoise is the political capital city, where all political and state institutions are based.

Dublin is now overcrowded, constrained by the Irish Sea on one side, and is very remote from the rest of the country. Portlaoise is in the centre of the country, with excellent road and rail infrastructure, and can expand in all directions. There is space here for a badly needed new airport, and state-of-the-art hospitals.

11. Ireland is a peaceful nation, and does not have an army. If Ireland is attacked by foreign forces, the Police will organise the citizens to defend the country, but a 75% referendum result will allow surrender.

An army is effectively a state-run murder machine, training soldiers to kill on sight. The Irish army at present is a scandalous waste of money. Peace-keeping missions are also a waste of money (and some valuable lives), when in fact diplomacy should be the preferred options. Irelands presence in some countries for decades has not solved any problems, only hidden them. For example, why should Ireland be involved in the Golan Heights in Syria, when Israel, backed by America, is well able to defend itself?

The present Army budget should be partly allocated to the Police, to provide better training, better salaries, more manpower, more equipment and hardware, and any balance used to reduce income tax. The fight against "drugs" requires zero tolerance and substantial investment in manpower and equipment.

12. Ireland is neutral in matters of war and conflict. Ireland will not allow any military aircraft or ship or personnel or equipment to stop or pass through Irish airspace or waters or land.

Ireland has failed in this regard in facilitating American military airplanes, when Britain is just a few miles further on, with which it shares a "special relationship", resulting from the massive loans America gave Britain during the Second World War.

13. Ireland does not allow the use of firearms (guns), except by the Police. Ireland does not manufacture guns or ammunition or any military equipment or supplies,

nor software, computers, electronic devices etc capable of military use or assistance.

Farmers do not need guns to control vermin, since traps or poison are equally effective.

14. The Euro is the national currency.

15. As Europeans, all road users in Ireland drive on the right-hand side.

16. The State means all the citizens of Ireland, and is not a separate body or institution. The Ministers and all civil and public servants are merely temporary representatives of the people, and shall not exercise power beyond that stated in this constitution, nor over-rule the rights of all citizens.

17. Ireland adheres to the relevant European and International laws.

Citizens Duties and Rights

18. The national motto of Ireland is: "I am proud to be Irish, and Ireland is proud of me."

19.   All permanent residents of Ireland are citizens, regardless of nationality, and must carry an Identity Card, renewable every five years. Those who wish to be identified as Irish for travel purposes may obtain an Irish Passport.

Identity cards, with current photograph, help to curtail fraud when claiming any free State service.

Citizen's Duties:

20.   To register as a voter from the age of 21, and thereafter to vote in all elections and referenda.

21.   To act as a good ambassador for Ireland when travelling outside the country.

22.   To respect the country, property, infrastructure, fellow citizens, temporary residents, and visitors.

23. To obey the laws, rules and regulations of Ireland, including taxation laws, and strive to abide by this Constitution.

24. To study and educate ourselves to the best of our ability, so as to become productive citizens, whether in industry, commerce , the professions, agriculture, or other useful pursuits.

25. To work to the best of our ability, for personal requirements, and, where possible in order to make the country a better place. This duty extends to working in Ireland for at least ten years during a working life, in gratitude for being raised and educated in Ireland.

26. To provide food, clothes, and a home for ourselves and any spouse and children, to the best of our ability, and to limit the number of any children according to our financial means.

27. The family is generally the backbone of Irish society, usually comprising a mother, father, and a child, while acknowledging that some couples have no children, and other families have same-sex parents. Single-parent families are acceptable, but the State will intervene if there is more than one child, and place any additional children in adoptive care. The State acknowledges that single people are also valuable citizens.

28.   Marriage is no longer a requirement to create a family.   However, if a child is born outside wedlock, a legally binding civil contract is deemed to have been executed, and both parents must record their names and addresses on the Birth Certificate. If the parents choose not to live together, they shall execute a Divorce Agreement, making provision for the new-born child and the spouse who will rear the child.

29.   To use all farmland and other property for productive purposes, and not allow it to lie idle, even if sub-letting necessary.

30.   Not to strike if the general public is adversely affected.

31. Use public transport in cities as far as possible, in order to reduce carbon emissions from cars.

Citizen's Rights:

32. Right to live in a fair and just society.

33. All citizens are equal. Companies, company directors and company shareholders shall not be afforded any greater rights than the ordinary citizen.

Hiding   behind   limited-liability   companies   is   not acceptable. The recent recession saw developers and builders liquidating their companies, owing billions of euros to individuals and small businesses, or the scandalous practice of them going to England to become bankrupt within a very short timeframe, and then re-appearing back in Ireland doing business again. Residential mortgage-holders meanwhile had to suffer in silence, having previously been strongly advised by the Taoiseach of the day that they would be better off committing suicide if they didn't buy a property with a 100% mortgage (sometimes even a 110% mortgage) being peddled by the un-regulated banking sector!

34. Freedom to practice any religion in private.

In the past, the State and the Catholic Church were inter-twined, although citizens could not elect church leaders. The Catholic Church controlled all schools and hospitals, and ruled with an iron fist, enforcing medieval rules and practices on the entire population, with only a few exceptions. Politicians did what the Catholic Church dictated, especially when the orders were given by the feared dictator himself, Archbishop John Charles McQuaid. In recent decades, the church hierarchy has been found to be hypocritical evil-doers, with child sexual abuse scandals, Magdalene laundries abuses, etc.

Religion has now fallen out of favour, but some laity still hold to their religious beliefs, and are entitled to practice ceremonies in private, but they must never again be allowed to influence or control the nation.

Churches, mosques, synagogues, and other places for public religious worship and assembly are acceptable, but must not display signs or banners, or emit sounds such as bells or calling to prayer, which might offend the general public, other religions or people of no religion.

35. Freedom of speech, in verbal and written form, subject to the rights of fellow citizens.

There is no right to abuse and offend individuals and groups of citizens, or to incite others to hatred or to riot.

36. Right to good name and reputation, without being slandered or defamed by others.

37. Freedom of movement around the country, and to travel in and out of the country.

38. Right to own property, both real and personal, with the overriding condition that the State is the ultimate owner of the country of Ireland, and can compulsorily purchase any land and building for State use, including use for schools, hospitals, offices, stores, roads, canals, railways, and other infrastructure, utilities, etc., or to facilitate the proper planning and development of the country, such as assisting private developers to assemble useful sites.

39. Right to a private life, without abuse or interference.

40. Right to the privacy of the home, unless the home is being used for un-lawful purposes.

41. Right to engage in peaceful and non-obstructive public assembly, for limited periods, subject to the rights of other citizens, both pedestrians and motorists, to go about their lives.

Marches, strikes, and protests are often designed to cause maximum annoyance and disruption to the general public, which is unacceptable in a civilised society. The various courts are provided to handle such issues, and must be used.

If a large space is needed for a public meeting, there are plenty of big public parks suitable for crowds, such as the Phoenix Park in Dublin, or big stadiums such as Croke Park in Dublin.

42. Right to form trade unions, for the purpose of engaging in private negotiations with employers.

43. Right of children to be properly educated without charge, from the age of four up to completion of the Leaving Certificate, or completion of Technical Education to obtain a trade or manual skill. Third Level education is available, without charge, following interview, to those capable of obtaining a professional qualification, depending on the needs of the country. Masters and Doctorates, if available, shall be fully payable by the student. The State does not provide student accommodation. School is compulsory for all children from the age of 4 to 12.

44. Right to medical and hospital treatment in case of serious accident or non-preventable disease or illness, paying according to means. Diseases related to smoking, alcohol, etc shall be relegated to second place, and penalised financially.

45. Right of all children to know from infancy who their biological parents are, and for their Birth Certificate to include the names and addresses and occupations of both parents.

At the moment, some unmarried mothers have babies with anonymous fathers, and later in life, there would be a risk of siblings marrying each other, with the potential for serious health risks to future offspring.

46. Right to marry above the age of sixteen, and divorce, subject to making the best provisions for the children under the age of 21. Bigamy is not permitted, whether within or outside marriage.

47. Right to obtain and use contraceptives, and right to an abortion in the early stages of pregnancy.

48. Right to be born in a healthy condition, with the best medical assistance in hospitals which are fully

operational and fully staffed 24-hours a day, and 365-days of the year.

There have been too many botched births in recent decades, as a result of negligent, inefficient and under-staffed maternity facilities, resulting in medical damage and deaths in new-born babies.

49. Right to die, without interference by hospitals, medical personnel, or the State.

50. Right to be paid a living wage by employers, in order to obtain food, clothing, and accommodation. The constitution recognises that employees are the backbone of business, and capital (money, finance, etc) is only of secondary importance.

Most citizens are well able to buy their own food and clothes, and would probably be ashamed to accept hand-outs from the State as a way of life. However, when it comes to a house or apartment, many people are unable to afford a mortgage or rent, generally because their wages are too low. Some employers pay low wages, partly in order to increase their own profits, or partly because they are not charging realistic prices for their products or services. Therefore, the State, at the expense of the majority of taxpayers, has to step in and subsidise the wages (by providing cheap accommodation), which effectively amounts to subsidising the profits of a handful of wealthy employers. This is unjust and non-democratic.

In the past, especially in the middle of the 20th century, the State built thousands of homes, generally called Council houses, and rented them to deserving people at modest amounts. In effect the majority of tax-payers subsidised a minority, simply because a handful of employers wanted to get rich. Gradually, more and more people regarded a cheap Council house as a "right" under the constitution, regardless of his wages.

Then the unthinkable happened: the State (in reality, some gombeen politician) decided to "ape" Britain, and sold off many of the Council houses (State assets) to the sitting tenants, at a "knock-down" price, who later sold them at a big profit, and in some cases went back on the housing waiting-list again!

Now in the 21st century, the State is too lazy to re-build up the stock of Council houses, and instead pays massive rents to private landlords (including wealthy institutional investors), under the Housing Assistance Provisions (HAP). The State itself should build a supply of Council houses, at a far cheaper cost than payments under the HAP scheme, and either sell or rent them to deserving families.

The fundamentals remain the same: workers are entitled to wages capable of funding a long-term mortgage, and people should be actively and continuously encouraged to be self-reliant and not dependant on the State for a roof over their heads. Furthermore, national planning policy must ensure that smaller/cheaper houses are built both by the State and private developers, and that building specifications do not have to be top-of-the-range.

51. Right not to be over-taxed by the State, but only in proportion to the individuals means and wealth, and only after paying for food, clothing and basic accommodation.

52. Right to State financial assistance for those who are sick, ill, disabled, infirm, old, retired, according to means.

53. Right to some temporary Government financial assistance for those who are temporarily unemployed, in return for doing National Service work during this period.

There should be no free "dole" money for able-bodied people, and instead those people should give back something in return. There are many public projects to be tackled, such as cleaning up river banks, weeding neglected flower beds in public parks, painting public areas, repairing footpaths, etc.

54. Right to some temporary State financial assistance for those who need to supplement their accommodation costs, subject to means.

55. Right to run private newspapers, television stations, radio stations, and other broadcast and media organisations. There is no State newspaper or broadcaster.

56. Right to free-of-charge, easy and fast access to the judicial courts, whether in criminal or civil matters.

The present criminal system allows hardened convicts to appeal decisions all the way to the Supreme Court, all at the expense of the State. On the other hand, ordinary citizens are effectively denied access to the civil courts because of the huge financial risk associated with having to pay extortionist fees to an army of solicitors and barristers. The civil courts need to be staffed by State legal employees (civil servants), so that any citizen or company can have a dispute resolved at no expense to themselves.

At present, only the Director of Public Prosecutions can initiate a legal action in the criminal courts. Citizens should be allowed to initiate such actions, with the active assistance of the State, in situations where the Police or the DPP have failed to take action.

57. Right to sue the State, free of charge, for acts and omissions leading to loss, injury or death.

Government of Country

58. Ireland is a non-political country, with no political parties or lobby groups. There are no politicians, but instead there are qualified and experienced specialist professionals.

59. Ireland is centrally governed by two independent but complimentary authorities, namely an elected Ministerial Authority, and an elected Legislation Authority, with different members on the two authorities, based in different headquarters in Portlaoise. There is no Local government, only an elected County Representative who reports to the Ministerial Authority, and who also has a vote in both the Ministerial Authority Objectives and Legislation Authority Programme.

60. Separate elections are held every three years at least, in order to elect the Ministerial Authority, and the Legislation Authority. The two authorities shall not be elected at the same time, and no person can be on both authorities at the same time.

61. At least 10% of the annual national budget shall automatically be allocated to the Legislation Authority, and any remaining balance transferred back to the national budget at the end of each year.

62. All elections and Referenda are administered by the Election Commission, comprising the collected members of both the Ministerial Selection Commission and the Legislation Selection Commission.

63. The members of both Authorities and the County Representatives shall be treated the same as all other citizens, and shall not have any legal "privilege" in relation to their statements or actions in their official capacity.

Ministerial Authority

64. The country is managed by a Ministerial Authority, consisting of five democratically-elected Ministers, working in the Ministerial Buildings in Portlaoise. The annual salary for each of the five Ministers shall be equal, and shall be no more than €1 million each, adjusted annually up or down pro-rata to net Gross Domestic Product (excluding inflation), of wholly-owned Irish companies, and disregarding foreign multi-nationals.

65. The Ministerial Authority consists of the Prime Minister, Business Minister, Infrastructure Minister, Health Minister, Finance Minister, collectively responsible for all five Ministerial Departments, but each department shall be managed by the relevant Minister.

66. All Ministerial Departments are located in Portlaoise, in fully-owned (that is, not leased) national property.

67. The Ministerial Authority shall hold office for a period of three years, unless at least three members voluntarily resign or are ordered to resign.

The five-member Ministerial Authority (Prime, Business, Infrastructure, Health, Finance) is elected by voters from a panel of 5 to 15 selected candidates, nominated by the Ministerial Selection Commission, with a maximum of three candidates for each Ministerial function.

68. Any Irish citizen can be a candidate to become a particular Minister at election time, provided:

(a) The citizen is at least 40-years of age, and

(b) Has resided in Ireland for at least 30-years before the election, and

(c) Has no criminal record, nor was the subject of adverse findings in any official investigation, and

(d) Has a current Tax Clearance Certificate from the Ministry of Finance, and

(e) Has successfully been vetted by the Ministerial Selection Commission, and has been included in the shortlist of top three candidates, taking into account, educational qualifications, professional qualifications, employment experience, and any other attributes necessary for the particular Ministerial position. All candidates shall have an appropriate professional qualification in Public Administration.

69. If there is no suitable candidate for a particular Ministry, the position shall be advertised in English-speaking countries, for a candidate of recent Irish ancestry.

The Ministerial Selection Commission must publish a full curriculum vitae (CV) booklet about the selected candidates, at least one week before the election, delivered to every household in the country.

70. The public can nominate a candidate, and if that person agrees to be so honoured, he may apply to the Ministerial Selection Commission to be included as a candidate.

71. High-ranking civil servants (at least Principal Officer grade) will be entitled to apply to the Ministerial Selection Commission.

Civil servants effectively run the country now, regardless of which politicians are voted in by the citizens. They know the system intimately, and exert enormous influence over politicians, even to the extent to being able to "hoodwink" new Ministers, especially "re-shuffled" Ministers. Even without a Government, the civil service carries on running the country, collecting taxes, and paying salaries to teachers, nurses, Police, etc. Therefore, senior civil servants could make very good Ministers under the proposed new Constitution, and must be actively encourages to run for the new Ministerial positions.

72. Each outgoing Minister will automatically be entitled to apply to be a candidate for re-election to any one Ministry, alongside new applicants, while still maintaining the maximum number of candidates at three per Ministry.

73. An election for any or each Ministerial position, shall be on the basis of the candidate with the most votes winning the particular position, provided that at least 66.66% of voters have not rejected the candidate. Each citizen has one vote, which can be applied to their favourite candidate on each ballot paper, or the vote can be split into two parts (66.66% for the favourite, and 33.34% for the second choice), or a maximum of three parts (50% for favourite, 33.33% for second choice, and 16.67% for the last choice). Therefore, for a Ministerial Election, there shall be five ballot papers, with a maximum of three names on each paper. The voter puts a "1" opposite their favourite candidate, and may also put a "2" and "3" opposite other favoured candidates, and later, the counters shall "weigh" the votes proportionally.

74. Voter turnout must be at least 66.66% of registered voters, otherwise another election shall be held.

75. If voters do not like any of the candidates, they leave the space on the ballot sheet blank as appropriate.

76. If any candidate receives at least 66.66% of blank spaces on ballot sheets, he/she shall be eliminated, and a new candidate chosen from the original short-list by the Ministerial Selection Commission.

77.   Voting shall take place in Polling Stations, temporarily located in public National or Secondary schools, only on weekends.

78.   If a majority (66.66%) of all 29 County Representatives so decide, but only after complaints from at least 1,000 voters in each of the 29 counties (at least 29,000), any individual Minister can be brought before the Supreme Court on charges of misconduct, negligence, incompetence or similar matters, and if found guilty, shall resign immediatly, after which fresh elections shall be held. Such Court action shall take precedence over all other Supreme Court cases, whether existing or pending, and both processed and decided within three months of the decision of the 29 County Representatives.

All five Ministers can be investigated and removed by this means, by five separate Supreme Court cases, thus allowing for the election of a totally new Ministerial Authority.

Ministerial Authority General Functions

79. There are two main interdependent Ministerial Authority functions:

(a) Annual Objectives and Annual Results, both financial and non-financial.

(b) Routine Management.

(a) The future Years Annual Objectives and the previous years Annual Results shall be published and approved by the Ministerial Authority, and 29 elected County Representatives (weighted by the respective populations), with voting rights in the proportions of 50% for the Ministers and 50% for the Representatives. Objectives shall include current expenditure, capital expenditure, and taxation, and shall be published one month prior to setting the following years Objectives. The Objectives and Results can only be passed by a 66.66% majority, with voting taking place in public.

If the Objectives and Results are not passed by a majority (66.66%), then they will be amended and redrafted and republished, for a further vote. Failure to pass in three votes within a three month period will amount to a failure of the Ministerial Authority, and fresh elections shall be called within one month to elect a new Ministerial Authority.

The Ministerial Authority will implement the Annual Objectives within the following year.

(b) The country should be collectively managed by five elected Ministers, namely the Prime Minister, Business Minister, Infrastructure Minister, Health Minister, and Finance Minister.   Their duties shall include implementation of the Annual Objectives.

Specific Ministerial Functions

Prime Minister

80. The Prime Minister is the public representative of Ireland, and attends important national and international events as a guest.

81. Chairs weekly meetings of the Ministerial Authority.

82. Manages all State property including civil service accommodation, schools, hospitals, etc., and historic sites.

The present Office of Public Works should be disbanded, as it is not fit for purpose, with little or no expertise in property management, valuation, surveying, architecture, engineering, etc, relying instead on expensive external consultants.

83. Manages the National Library, National Museum, National Gallery, National Archives.

84. Makes quarterly (every three months) broadcast address to the country, outlining current issues and results, with the written speech posted to every household.

85.   Manages foreign policy.   Appoints overseas ambassadors, and welcomes foreign ambassadors. Ireland does not give direct financial aid to any "Third World" country, but instead, sends doctors, teachers, farmers, industrialists etc overseas on temporary assignment to assist development, and assist in famine relief.   Ireland promotes peace and mediation in troubled countries.

Ministry of Business

Employment

86.   Strongly fostering native Irish companies, small, medium and large, and encouraging exports of their products on a global scale.

Many well-educated young Irish people emigrate, and become very successful on foreign soil, which is a terrible loss to Ireland. Such people should be actively "head-hunted", and their talents and ambitions fostered inside Ireland.

87. Restricting foreign owned companies to a maximum of 25% of GDP.

Ireland is seriously over-reliant on "Foreign Direct Investment", i.e. multi-nationals setting up business in Ireland to avail of a low corporate tax rate, and to gain entry to the European Union market. When these two factors change, the foreign companies will disappear overnight. Irish employees in these foreign companies should be targeted and encouraged to set up their own businesses, using their acquired skills.

88.   Membership of the European Union for trade purposes only.

89.   All companies have permanent employees on the Board of Directors, with 50% of the voting rights.

90.   All companies allocate at least 50% of the annual profits to their employees, in addition to their salaries.

91.   Regulating the Agriculture and Fisheries sectors, and strongly promoting alternative use of agricultural land.

As a small island country, Ireland cannot afford to waste finite land resources on raising cows and cattle for export, when the space could be more profitably used for manufacturing. Ireland does not need to be self-sufficient in foodstuffs, and already imports most of its fruit and vegetables. Vast tracts of land lie idle, which should be confiscated by the State, and leased to young citizens anxious to start a manufacturing business.

92.   Marketing Ireland as a tourist destination, and regulating accommodation and restaurants.

The State has failed to regulate Airbnb, which allows anyone to rent their house or apartment to tourists.

The State does not financially support sport, such as football, swimming, greyhound racing, horse racing, arts, all of which are private hobbies.

Education

93. All schools and colleges are State-owned and run, and the State shall not assist or support any private schools or colleges.

At present the State pays the salaries of all teachers in the country, even those in so-called private schools. In the latter, the parents simply pay a small annual fee for additional facilities such as sports and other non-essential subjects.

The State should force the religious orders who currently own most of the schools in the country to sell them for a nominal sum of money, failing which all funding for salaries should be stopped immediately.

Irish and Latin should not be taught. For over 100-years, the Irish language has been "rammed down the throats" of Irish citizens, especially in schools, and in making it a requirement for entry to the civil and public service, but it is still a dead language. A vast fortune of money has been wasted in making road signs bi-lingual, printing official documents in Irish and English (doubling the cost), setting up Irish-speaking radio and television stations, etc.

Schools must place more emphasis on training for future employment.

94. All Primary Schools are equal, with males and females being educated together, with a legal obligation to teach all pupils the 3-R'S – reading, writing and arithmetic.

At present, many Irish citizens cannot read nor write, even though they passed through the school system. Hence, "NALA" was set up to teach adults to read and write, which is a poor reflection on the standard of teaching in Primary Schools.

Much better teacher training and initial vetting is required, and Continuous Professional Development throughout their careers. Poor or lazy teachers should be weeded out and dismissed at an early stage, before they can cause damage to pupils.

Pupils should not have to seek "grinds" from the black-market, because their school has failed them.

95. All Second-Level schools are equal, with males and females being educated together, offering a mixture of courses, both trade and professional, and linked to business and Third-Level colleges, taking into account the immediate , short-term, and long-term employment needs of the country.

96. All Third-Level education establishments are equal, and called Universities, offering a practical education, leading to a useful career. There are no courses in Arts, Politics, Social Science etc. Every major town in Ireland has a small sized University, limited to productive education, and not sport.

97. All schools and universities shall operate from 10.30am – 3.30pm, Monday to Friday, with one month Summer holidays, and one week holiday at Christmas, plus the usual Bank Holidays. Holidays are not allowed for religious events or festivities.

These hours are designed to curb traffic congestion at peak morning and evening commuting times.

98. Education is generally compulsory in Primary Schools, and then up to the Intermediate Certificate in Secondary schools.

Practical skills-based education is of paramount importance, and academic education is of little or no importance. Education should produce citizens ready for a varied and dynamic workforce, capable of starting or participating in every kind of business, whether technology, manufacturing, agriculture, financial services, etc, and proficient in foreign languages to enable export of products and services to all parts of the world.

Many students who are practically minded and talented "with their hands" have been misled into thinking that a University degree will lead to a fulfilling life, and instead find themselves in a rut, or unemployed, and meanwhile the State has to employ hundreds of thousands of non-English-speaking immigrants for the construction industry, hospitals, tourism, etc. The State needs to be self-sufficient, and provide its native citizens with the means to a productive and satisfying life.

Ministry of Infrastructure

Buildings

99. The Planning Board grants all Planning Permissions, and makes regulations for all building work, but leaves implementation to the designers, and the Courts.

There is practically no real planning in Ireland, only "red-tape" and short-term stunted vision. Housing estates consist of rows and rows of identical semi-detached houses (or "half-houses" as some see it), with colourless finishes. County councils made a shambles of planning, with zoning scandals, allegations of bribery and corruption, etc. During the "Celtic Tiger" era (1996 to 2007), large housing estates and blocks of apartments were built in tiny villages and towns all over Ireland, which became "ghost estates" and later had to be demolished. Stand-alone housing estates should be banned, and all residential buildings should be part of a varied mix of different-sized bungalows, two and three storey houses, small and larger apartment blocks, intermingled with shops, supermarkets, schools, community halls, sports centres, playing pitches, offices, factories, warehouses, etc. Initially all such developments should be centred on existing villages, towns, and cities. Ireland has a grey climate for much of the year, and colour should be a big factor in the streetscape, e.g. vibrant strong colours for roof tiles and slates, windows, doors, plasterwork etc, so that every residence is different and lively, reflecting Irish artistic and literary inclinations..

Expensive vanity projects ruined Victorian streetscapes during the recession of 2008 – 2015, such as the enormous hollow shell of a useless central library in Dun Laoghaire.

O'Connell Street in Dublin, supposedly the most important street in the country, is a national disgrace because of poor planning and control, and is merely a "rat-run" for buses and trams, and only acts as a means for getting to the more imposing side street, Henry Street. O'Connell Street should be full of smart department stores, cinemas, restaurants, etc, with lush trees and shrubs, making it a stand-alone destination to be proud of. Instead, the only department store (Clerys) was suddenly shut done by developers, and all that is left on the street is a multitude of fast-food outlets, a few small shops, one or two slot-machine businesses, one cinema, one hotel which was recently partly used for "homeless families", and bleak, hard landscaping with a British-designed tall steel pole masquerading as a "work of art". The pole stands on the site of the much loved Nelsons Pillar, with its panoramic viewing platform at the top, which was only partly damaged by an IRA bomb in 1966, and then completely demolished/blown-up by the city godfathers, instead of being repaired and a statue of Patrick Pearse provided on top, and renamed Pearse Pillar.

There is no need for development plans or zoning, since market forces and the Planning Board will ensure sensible planning. When a developer wants to build an estate of houses, for example, he approaches the Planning Board, who compulsory buys up the land at current market value for the existing use (e.g. farmland), and the Board sells the land on a long lease at cost price to the developer. The developer cannot hoard the land, but can sell it back to the Board if the scheme does not proceed.

All houses should have back gardens at least 20 metres long, and communal bleak open spaces should not be permitted.

The Board also buys land for the State to build Council houses.

100. All buildings, structures, and street furniture, over one hundred years old, are automatically Protected Structures, and cannot be demolished or altered without Planning Permission.

101. All one-off houses, and one-off apartment blocks up to four stories, and all extensions to them, are exempt from Planning, but must be certified upon completion by

a registered architect in respect of design and construction.

102. All housing estates, groups of apartment blocks over three storeys, and commercial buildings, and all extensions to them, are designed, supervised, and certified by a registered architect, once approved by the Planning Board.

Ireland never had a housing rental market before the Celtic Tiger era, and apartments were initially intended for temporary immigrant workers. No more should be built, and developers must build houses with garden space. If developers do not build dwellings, the State should build a range of house types on State-owned land, such as most of the Phoenix Park, army barracks, etc., and sell them to citizens at cost price, or rent some of them to poorer people.

Golf clubs in cities are a scandalous waste of scarce land resources, and should be acquired by the State at a nominal fee, for building houses.

103. The Central Housing Agency allocates Council houses in every county. Tenants must go where sent, even outside their existing county, or be removed from the waiting-list.

Many dwellings built during the Celtic Tiger years in rural towns and villages, including "ghost estates", are now owned by the State, but some are empty or under-utilised.

In the past, older council houses and apartments were rented to large families, but now that the children have left home, the parents should be allocated smaller dwellings, ideally in the same neighbourhood, and the larger dwelling rented to another larger family.

Transport.

104. All roads, railways, airports, ports, are State-owned.

105. The main city-centres are pedestrian-only, accessed via public buses and trams, taxis, and motorcycles, supported by free-of-charge multi-storey carparks on the periphery, whether below or above ground. Buses shall run in concentric circles, in addition to the present arterial arrangement.

106. Public transport in the main cities is paramount, and no private cars are permitted within the city limits during the morning and evening rush hours.

No need for bus lanes, since all cars will be banned from the bus network during rush hours.

No need for cycle lanes, since bicycles banned in cities and towns. Cycle lanes are a great waste of public money, since they are seldom used, slow down vehicles, and are often ignored by cyclists, who still prefer to obstruct the adjoining road and bus lanes. Cycling is the poor-man's mode of transport, harking back to a by-gone more leisurely era, and has no place in modern cities and towns. Motorcycles are allowed because they share the road with cars, and pay road tax.

Commuters from outside the city centres should use public transport to gain access to workplaces and shops.

Speed limits on all secondary rural roads must be reduced to a maximum of 60-80 kilometres, to prevent excessive deaths on such roads.

Utilities

107. The State owns all networks and systems supplying electricity, gas, water, sewerage, and broadband. Broadband is charged on usage only, similar to electricity and gas. Electricity is substantially generated from wave power, utilising the never-ending sea-currents which surrounds our island.

Local Management

108. Each county has a small local office, and the Manager attends monthly progress meetings with the Ministry in Portlaoise.

109. The 29 County Representatives brief the Ministry at monthly meetings in Portlaoise, on any issues requiring the attention of the Ministerial Authority.

Ministry of Health & Public Assistance

Health

110. The State owns and manages all Public Hospitals, and Local Mini-Hospitals.

The State should force the "almost-obsolete" religious orders who currently own most of the hospitals in the country to sell them for a nominal sum of money, failing which all funding for salaries should be stopped immediately.

The existing Health Services Executive (HSE) should cease business immediately, since it is simply one giant useless bureaucratic machine, hindering the great work of doctors and nurses. In effect, the HSE is a duplication of the Department of Health, one in a massive headquarters in Naas, and the other in an even bigger headquarters in Dublin, both blaming each other for being lethargic! For example, neither set of civil servants will accept responsibility for making a shambles of the Cervical Screening project. In the past, hospitals were run by nuns in a highly efficient manner, but now there are no more nuns, except a handful of retired sisters. Surely, there are lay people who have similar skills to nuns?

Consultants should only work in either the public or private sector, but not both. Nurses and ancillary staff should be much better paid, in order to improve morale and productivity. It is a national disgrace that the present system relies so heavily on foreign-trained doctors and nurses, when our own education system produces better graduates who are forced to emigrate.

111. Alcohol is only available from Chemist Shops in rationed and very limited quantities for medicinal purposes, and is not available in any other outlet, e.g. Not in Public Houses, Supermarkets, Shops, Off-Licences.

Chemists can advise on safe levels of alcohol intake, and number of units in each bottle or can. Nowadays, chemists sell everything from beauty products to Christmas presents, birthday cards, etc, and even tablets to take for a "hangover". Therefore, they are ideally positioned to safely dispense alcohol.

112. Smoking of tobacco, and use of nicotine products, is forbidden in Ireland.

Currently, the Government recoups a large amount of tax from sales of cigarettes, but then has to spend much more on hospital treatment for lung cancer, etc.

113. Gambling is forbidden in Ireland.

Going to the "bookies" is a pastime for those who can least afford to lose money.

Public Assistance

114. The State pays pensions to those over the age of 65, other than people who have company or private pensions. Civil and public servants shall be treated the same as all other citizens.

115. The State assists financially those unable to work, because of sickness, ill-health, disability, or temporary unemployment, the latter engaging in Community Service while receiving assistance.

Ministry of Finance

116. Minister must have a strong background in finance, accountancy, and economics.

117. The ministry runs the Central Bank.

118. The ministry collects annual taxes.

Income and similar taxes shall be no more than:

Up to €25,000 (free of any tax), €26,000 - €50,000 (10%), €51,000 - €75,000 (20%), €76,000 - €100,000 (30%), €101,000 - €500,000 (35%), €501,000 - €1million (45%), over €1million (50%).

Every employed citizen shall pay income tax at these maximum rates, regardless of the source of income. Part-time citizens who spend only some of their time in Ireland, shall be taxed pro-rata to the number of days they sleep in Ireland, and shall provide evidence of all their income worldwide.

The present Childrens Allowance should only be paid to needy people, instead of to all parents regardless of income.

119. The State can only borrow money for <u>major</u> capital projects, and the total cumulative borrowings is restricted to a maximum of 10% of Gross Domestic Product.

120. Capital gains shall be taxed as income, and the family home shall be so taxed when a person dies.

121. Multi-national companies are not allowed to have non-productive headquarters in Ireland, unless they are fully taxed on all income passing through their books, since Ireland is not a tax haven for the rich.

The existing tax system is much too complicated and unfair, resulting in a large "black economy", and elaborate tax-avoidance schemes dreamed up by accountants and tax-specialists. However, because of excessive taxation of the lower and middle income groups, the Government feels it can waste money on a bloated civil service, unnecessary projects, gross inefficiency in all departments, etc.

Lobbying

122.   Private and group lobbying of Ministers and officials is strictly prohibited. All lobbying is public, via written submissions, published immediately on the relevant websites.

123.   Ministers may invite submissions, by letter or online, but all submissions have to be published immediately online on the Authorities website.

County Management

124. Ireland has no Local Government, but each county has a sub-office of the Ministry of Infrastructure, with a full-time manager, and small support staff, operating from a small office in each main county city or town. The manager is fully answerable to the Ministry, and makes monthly reports on progress and local issues.

At present, county council staff are answerable to no one, and only suit themselves, whilst ignoring the concerns of citizens.

125. The County Management has no Planning function whatsoever.

County Councils have been hotbeds of corruption for decades, because of the potential for financial or similar rewards when agricultural land is re-zoned by councillors for use as housing or industrial estates. Interference in individual Planning Permissions has also brought councils into disrepute. At present, An Bord Pleanala in Dublin effectively decides on all major and important planning issues, and also too many petty domestic issues.

126. There are no Commercial Rates nor Local Property Tax.

Commercial rates are a very unjust tax, based on historic rental values, and applied even in times of recession. Any such rates should be levied on profits. Instead of low corporate taxation, companies should be taxed the same as individuals, bringing in more revenue for the country. Local Property Tax is also very unjust, and instead, only income derived from property usage should be taxed.

127.   Each county sub-office is responsible for maintenance of public lighting, street cleaning, minor road maintenance, libraries, free car parking, public toilets.

County councils, in conjunctions with local politicians, have wasted billions of euros on ring-roads and by-passes in the remotest parts of Ireland, while on the other hand, the National road network and rail network has not been properly developed or upgraded.

Councils no longer collect domestic and commercial waste, and instead have passed-the-buck to a multitude of profitable private operators. Now you can find three or four different companies calling to the same housing estate to collect waste. The multitude of different coloured domestic bins are a blight on the street-scape, similar to the days when every house had an ugly TV aerial on the roof. Instead, every road should have a few well-placed large "wheelie-bins" where citizens deposit their waste, similar to the arrangements in apartment blocks.

The councils do little in the way of street cleaning, and instead rely on the privately-sponsored Tidy Towns organisation to keep Ireland clean and tidy, in addition to locals volunteers who clean their housing estates once or twice a year. Instead, the city councils spend their time collecting dog poo from public waste bins, instead of making the dog-owners flush the poo down their own toilets.

Car parking should be free, and so encourage more shoppers and visitors. At present, it amounts to a self-serving charity collection.

There should be a lot more public toilets, single booth style, with a small charge to prevent anti-social behaviour. At present, citizens and visitors have to rely on the goodwill of public houses.

County Representative

128.   There is no Local Government in Ireland, and therefore no councillors. However, there is one County Representative elected every year, who acts solely a conduit for communication between the county citizens and the Minister for Infrastructure. The Representative exercises no local power, but has a vote in both the Ministerial Authority and the Legislation Authority for specific objectives.

129. There are monthly public meetings in each county to brief the County Representative about local issues. Minutes of all such meetings are published within a fortnight, and delivered to all homes in the county. Citizens can also write to the Representative, via a public website.

130.   The County Representatives attend monthly meetings with the Minister for Infrastructure.   The minutes of such meetings are published within a fortnight, and delivered to all homes in each county.

131. The County Representative has a small office in the main town or city of each county, but it is separate from the sub-office of the Ministry.

132. Representative are paid a fixed salary amounting to no more than 10% of a Ministers salary.

133. County Representatives are elected annually, from three candidates nominated by the Ministerial Selection Commission, using the same criteria for the selection of Ministers. Outgoing Representative are entitled to be on the ballot paper, and re-elected no more than ten times.

134. County Representatives can be sacked by the Ministerial Selection Commission after investigation for negligence, incompetence, etc, if at least 1,000 random voters in a county complain.

Legislation Authority

135.   New and amending legislation is decided by a Legislation Authority of six democratically-elected full-time Legislators, working in the Legislation Buildings in Portlaoise.

136. The annual salary for each of the six Legislators shall be equal, and each shall be no more than 50% of the salary for a Minister.

137. The Legislation Authority shall be made up of three legal personnel and three lay people, elected every three years, and nominated by the Legislation Selection Committee.

138. The six-member team is elected by voters from a panel of 6 to 18 selected candidates.

139. Any Irish citizen can be a candidate to become a member of the Authority at election time, provided:

(a) The citizen is at least 40-years of age, and

(b) Has resided in Ireland for at least 30-years before the election, and

(c)   Has no criminal record, nor was the subject of adverse findings in any official investigation, and

(d) Has a current Tax Clearance Certificate from the Ministry of Finance, and

(e) Has successfully been vetted by the Legislation Selection Commission, and has been included in the shortlist of top three candidates, taking into account, educational qualifications, professional qualifications, employment experience, and any other attributes necessary for the particular position. All legal candidates shall have an appropriate professional qualification.

140. The Legislation Authority deals with its own budget, but not the national budget.

141. The future Annual Programme and the previous years Results shall be published and approved by the Legislation Authority, the Ministerial Authority, and the 29 elected County Representatives (weighted by the respective populations), with voting rights in the proportions of 50% for the Legislation Authority, 25% for the Ministerial Authority, and 25% for the Representatives. The Annual Programme shall comprise new legislation and amendments to existing legislation, including Statutory Instruments, Regulations, etc., and shall be published one month prior to setting the following years Programme. The Programme and Results can only be passed by a 66.66% majority, with voting in public.

If the Programme and Results are not passed by a majority (66.66%), then they will be amended and redrafted and re-published, for a further vote. Failure to pass in three votes within a three month period will amount to a failure of the Legislation Team, and fresh elections shall be called within one month to elect a new Legislation Team.

The Legislation Authority will implement the Annual Programme within the following year.

Legislation approved by the Authority shall be immediately entered on the Statute Books, and sent to the Ministerial Authority for immediate implementation, unless contrary to the Ministerial Authorities Objectives or this Constitution.

142.   The Legislation Authority considers any written submission from any County Representatives, and publishes these submissions.

143.   The Legislation Authority considers any written submissions from any Court, and publishes these submissions.

144.   The Legislation Authority considers any written submissions from Ministers, and publishes these submissions.

145. The Legislation Authority considers any written submissions from individual voters, and publishes these submissions.

Administration of Justice

146. Both police and courts are an integrated public service managed by the Legislation Authority, working closely together to uphold the laws made by the Authority and its predecessors, maintain public order, preserve peace, convict criminal suspects, punish convicts, and resolve commercial and personal disputes. All personnel and staff are appointed by the Public & Civil Service Recruitment Agency.

The present separation of these two organisations is very inefficient, and wasteful of resources, sometimes leading to Police cases being thrown out of Court because of some minor technicality. Judges and lawyers need to be more actively involved in cases, visiting sites and scenes, instead of being shielded in their "ivory towers".

Police Corps

147. The size of the police corps shall be at least 0.005% of the gross population, being a mixture of male and female according to needs.

148. All entrants to the police corps shall be at least 21 years of age, and undergo a 2-year full time sandwich course of instruction and practical training, with supplementary courses as the police officers progress up the ranks.

149. The majority of police officers shall not bear firearms, except those on special duty facing criminals who are armed, in which case the officer should only shoot to disarm the suspect, and not to kill him.

150. The large number of police on the "beat" in cities and towns is designed to eliminate anti-social behaviour, reduce the incidence of crime, catch criminals, collect local "intelligence, and foster goodwill in communities.

151. The Police Corps incorporates Mountain Rescue, and the National Lifeboat Service.

These vital services should not be left to volunteers, because it is the State responsibility to provide a well-funded organisation.

152. The Police Corps includes shipping patrols, and air patrols.

Courts of Justice

153. This vital service comprises the Criminal Courts, Civil Courts, Arbitration Forum, Court of Enquiry, Citizens Court, and the Complaints Adjudicator.

154. The Criminal courts comprise the Supreme Court, Court of Criminal Appeal, Central Criminal Court (equivalent to the High Court), Circuit Court, District Court, in descending order of seniority. The Special Criminal Court deals with national security issues, and is similar to the Central Criminal Court.

155. The Civil courts comprise the Supreme Court, Court of Appeal, High Court, Circuit Court, and District Court.

156. The Arbitration Forum comprises a panel of commercial experts in different specialities, such as accountancy, engineering, construction, etc, and hears cases in private in a semi-informal manner, and the arbitrators published findings are final and legally binding.

157. The Court of Enquiry, presided over by a three-judge panel, makes investigations into matters of public concern, and issues non-binding Reports, which might form the basis for criminal prosecutions.

These matters were dealt with by very expensive and slow Tribunals in the past.

158. The Citizens Court, sitting in Galway city, comprises twelve citizens chosen annually at random from the voters register, sitting (if necessary) at least once a year to hear complaints (if any) about any elected person, only in circumstances where:

If at least 66.66% of County Representatives fail to agree to take Supreme Court action,

and

If at least 1,000 random people on the voters register from all 29 county councils, that is, at least 29,000 random voters, complain about any of the elected County Representatives, or about any of the five Ministers, or any of the six Legislators,

then

he/she is summoned before the Citizens Court, and may be immediately removed from office if found guilty by at least a 75% majority, or given 3-months to redeem himself/herself.

159. The Complaints Adjudicator decides on complaints about the performance or non-performance of civil service functions, heard in private, but the general results are published annually, while not revealing the names or address of the civil servants.

Politicians and county councillors waste most of their time on local constituency matters, instead of dealing with national issues. The Complaints Adjudicator would fulfil that role much more effectively, and with full transparency.

160. The Family Law Court handles divorce cases, and sits in private, although general results are published annually, while not revealing the names and addresses of the parties.

161.   The Childrens Court, held in private, handles criminal allegations against children under the age of sixteen. General results are published annually, while not revealing the names and addresses of the parties.

162. The Labour Court handles workers disputes, and hears cases in private, although the outcomes are binding and published immediately.

163. There are no juries in any Court.

The outmoded system of selecting twelve citizens at random is a bizarre arrangement, designed to enhance the theatrical performance of the judges and barristers. The judges and barristers are trained and experienced legal professionals, and only they know the complexities of the law. Most lay people, both well-educated and poorly-educated citizens, are ignorant of legal technicalities, and not qualified or experienced enough to pass judgement. The mere fact of a hierarchy of Courts means that many mistakes are even made by the trained judges in the lower courts, which have to be Appealed to higher Courts. The time is long overdue when judges have to be "judgemental" and make decisions, instead of "passing the buck" to unqualified and baffled juries. Judges should no longer regard their role as "master of ceremonies" in the courtroom.

164. One judge decides cases in each District Court and each Civil Court, and a panel of three judges decides cases in all higher Courts. All judges are civil servants, and dress in respectable attire, without any theatrical wigs and gowns.

165. Only lawyers employed by the State present and defend cases in all Courts, and dress in respectable attire, without any theatrical wigs and gowns.

At present, the State prosecutes crimes with its own lawyers (comprising solicitors who are State employees, and barristers who are self-employed), and with free legal aid, defendants also use State lawyers.

Civil cases should be the same, with State lawyers on both sides. Or alternatively, anyone who wishes can use the Arbitration Forum, with State arbitrators, but private experts on both sides. Or, alternatively, go completely private to an independent Arbitrator.

The legal profession is currently very inefficient and extremely expensive, with desk-bound solicitors working for the State or in private practice, and barristers doing all the talking in the Courtroom, and being self-employed. A single profession of "lawyer" is long overdue to perform the joint role of solicitor and barrister.

166. "Precedent" is not binding in Irish Courts, but may be quoted in lawyers arguments.

"Precedent" (the judgements in previous similar court cases) allows judges to "pass the buck", and prevents progressive and enlightened judges from using their own intelligence, training and experience. Hence, the entire Court system becomes stagnant, unjust, and merely a "rubber-stamping" exercise.

167. The Courts adhere generally to sentencing guidelines, so that two similar crimes in different parts of the country have broadly similar outcomes.

168. Compensation awards for loss and injury adhere to general guidelines.

169. The "Media" (newspapers, broadcasters, etc) is not permitted to report <u>during</u> any Court case, including criminal trials, whether within or outside the Court precincts, but can publish when the trial is finished.

170. The "media" and general public are permitted to be observers in public Court cases, but only from behind soundproof glass screens, and via audio equipment.

Courtrooms need to be quiet and dignified, with no distractions from outsiders, and less likelihood of lawyers "playing to the gallery".

Prisons

171. Many crimes are dealt with by means of substantial financial fines, which are intended to punish the criminal and deter any repeat offence, and can be paid off over any number of years.

172. Dangerous criminals, who are a continuing danger to the public, are imprisoned for a period in Mental Hospitals, and treated appropriately.

173. Labour Camps, located in remote places and not in the cities or towns, are provided for those convicted of serious crimes, and in need of rehabilitation. They are divided into male and female camps, with separate camps for offenders under the age of 16, those between 17 and 30, those between 31 and 60, and those over 61. The camps function as manufacturing facilities, offering skills training to suitable candidates, operating a 40-hour week. The goods are sold to the public at market value, and net profits allocated to the prisoners.

Prisons are de-moralising institutions, tending to harden and embitter the inmates. Useful employment and occupations in Labour Camps are definitely therapeutic, and provide a humane environment in preparations for re-introduction back into civilian life.

Referendum

174. The Legislation Authority shall hold a public Referendum if it considers that this Constitution needs to be amended or extended, and at least a 66.66% majority vote will be sufficient to allow the amendment or extension, provided that there has been at least a 66.66% turnout of the electorate.

175. Any member of the electorate may apply directly to the Legislation Authority for the Constitution to be amended or changed by a Referendum, and the request and decision shall be published within six months.

176. This constitution shall be re-drafted every 25-years, in order to keep up to date, even if only minor modifications are needed.

Election Commission

177.   The Election Commission comprises the six members of the Ministerial Selection Commission and the six members of the Legislation Selection Commission, and meets at least annually in a separate office in Portlaoise.

178.   The Commission organises all elections and referenda, and publishes the results, in addition to sending the written results to all households in the country.

179.   The Commission compiles and updates the list of all voters in the country. Any citizen over the age of 21 who wishes to vote, applies to be included in this list, and may also ask to be removed from the list. Citizens emigrating or not wishing to vote, must advise the Election Commission, so that voter turnout at elections and referenda can be accurately calculated, and to prevent fraudulent voting.

180.   The Commission issues a free copy of this Constitution, and any future amendments, to every existing and future household in the country.

Many citizens have never read the Constitution, or else, have forgotten its contents.

Ministerial Selection Commission

181. This Selection Commission consists of the managing or senior partner from two Accountancy firms, two senior civil or public servants (at least Principal Officer grade), and two lay members.

182. The names of all willing Accountancy firms, all higher grade public and civil servants, and all registered voters, shall be entered into a public annual Lottery, in order to appoint the annual Selection Commission.

183. The Selection Commission, sitting in an independent State building in Portlaoise, will advertise the Ministerial position, or County Representative position, and invite and interview applicants from suitably qualified persons.

184. A majority (66.66% at least) of Commission members shall select the candidates to be presented to the voters for the five Ministerial roles, and 29 County Representatives.

185. The members of the Commission shall be appointed in an honorary capacity, with no salary.

Legislation Selection Commission

186. This Selection Commission consists of the managing or senior partner from two Lawyers firms, one senior civil or public servant (at least Principal Officer grade), one High Court judge, and two lay members.

187. The names of all willing Lawyers firms, all higher grade civil and public servants, all High Court judges, and all registered voters, shall be entered into a public annual Lottery, in order to appoint the annual Selection Commission.

188. The Selection Commission, sitting in an independent State building in Portlaoise, will advertise the Legislation Authority position, and invite and interview applicants from suitably qualified persons.

189. A majority (66.66% at least) of Commission members shall select the candidates to be presented to the voters for the six Legislation Team positions.

190. The members of the Commission shall be appointed in an honorary capacity, with no salary.

Public & Civil Service Recruitment Agency

191.   Public servants means those State workers who interface with the general public, including police, courts (including judges), hospital workers, teachers, fire service, etc.

192. Civil servants means those State workers who have little or no interface with the general public, such as office workers in the various Government departments.

193.   This Agency consists of the managing or senior partner from one Accountancy firm or specialist Recruitment firm, one Lawyer firm, one Minister, one senior civil servant (at least Principal Officer grade), one senior public servant, and one lay member.

194.   The names of all willing Accountancy firms or specialist Recruitment firms, Lawyer firms, all higher grade public and civil servants, all Ministers, and all registered voters, shall be entered into a public annual Lottery, in order to appoint the annual Recruitment Agency.

195. The Agency, sitting in an independent State building in Portlaoise, will advertise the Public or Civil Service

position, invite and interview applicants from suitably qualified persons, and appoint successful candidates.

196.   In respect of all senior appointments and promotions, including all Judges, police superintendents, hospital managers, school principals, ranks including and above Principal Officer in the Civil Service, etc., a majority (66.66% at least) of Agency members shall select the candidates to be employed.

Senior civil servants need to be accountable to the citizens of Ireland, and therefore all initial appointments and important promotions need to be properly controlled and monitored.

197. The Agency regulates all civil and public servants, including dismissal of staff, under the same rights and obligations as the private sector.

Traditionally, the Civil Service attracted un-ambitious rural people, with the promise of an easy job for life, and a guaranteed generous pension after a few decades of employment. Except for a basic Leaving Certificate (including the mandatory Irish!), educational qualifications were not necessary, and promotion was guaranteed as you got older. Rural politicians and county councillors, with a parochial agenda, found such employees easy to manipulate, with sweet talk of the county football results. The Civil Service became bloated, stagnant, inefficient and incompetent, resulting in huge financial loss to tax-payers. Using the maximum "sick leave" has now become "an entitlement" amongst healthy but lazy staff. Anecdotal evidence suggests that at least 50% of workers could be dismissed without any adverse effects on the service, but it seems that there are no dismissal or disciplinary procedures. The civil service now needs to be down-sized, re-organised and operated like any big business, such as banking.

The End

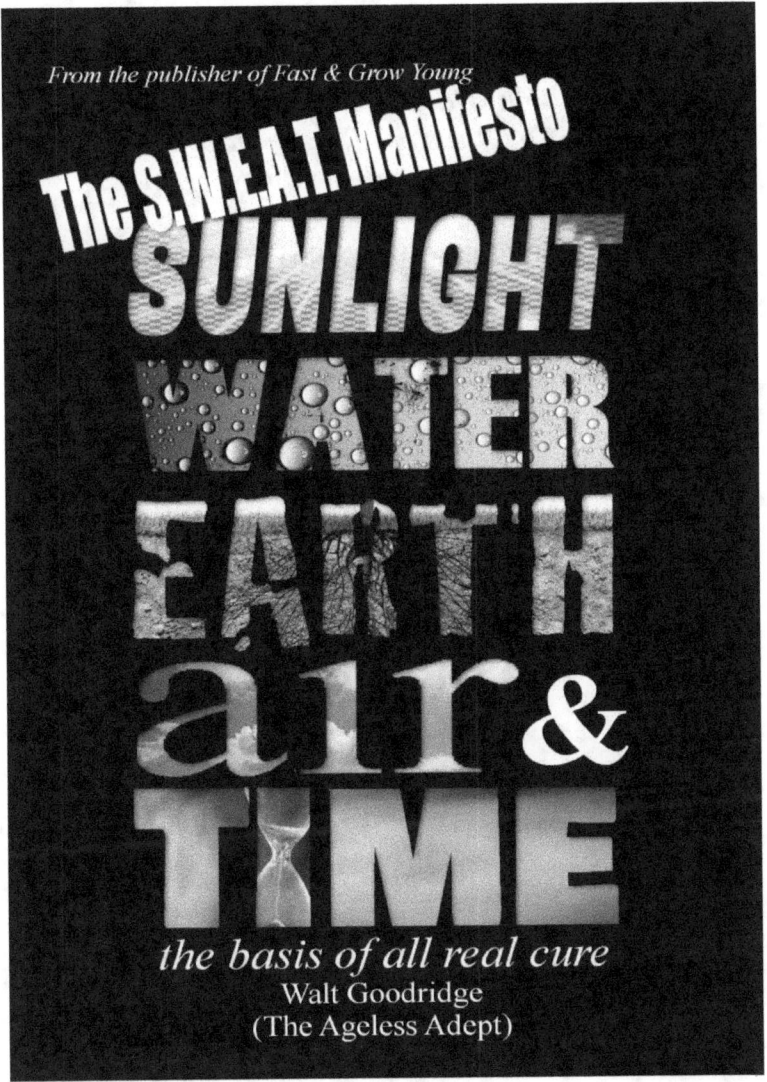

From the publisher of Fast & Grow Young

The S.W.E.A.T. Manifesto

SUNLIGHT
WATER
EARTH
air &
TIME

the basis of all real cure

Walt Goodridge
(The Ageless Adept)

The S.W.E.A.T Manifesto:
Sunlight, Water, Earth, Air & Time
The Basis of All <u>Real</u> Cure
(Volume 2 in the Ageless Adept™ Series)

© Walt F.J. Goodridge. All rights reserved.

Published by Walt F.J. Goodridge
dba a company called W
ISBN-13: 9781095420577

Visit a store called W

Books, apps, audio, video, merchandise,
courses, Walt's passion projects, freebies
and more from a company called W!
www.waltgoodridge.com/store

Distributed by
The Passion Profit Company
(646) 481-4238
sales@passionprofit.com

Educational institutions, government agencies, libraries and corporations are invited to inquire about quantity discounts. Contact: sales@passionprofit.com

Printed in the United States of America